MW00513209

Bread Machine Cookbook: Quick and Easy Recipes for Homemade Bread. Step-by-Step Guide for Baking With Any Bread Maker.

Susan Williams

Table of Contents

Fruit Breads

Banana Bread

Preparation Time: 1 hour 40 minutes

Cooking time: 40- 45 minutes

Servings: 1 loaf

Ingredients:

- 1 teaspoon Baking powder
- 1/2 teaspoon Baking soda
- 2 bananas, peeled and halved lengthwise
- 2 cups all-purpose flour
- 2 eggs
- 3 tablespoon Vegetable oil
- 3/4 cup white sugar

Directions:

1. Put all the Ingredients in the bread pan. Select dough setting. Start and mix for about 3-5 minutes.
2. After 3-5 minutes, press stop. Do not continue to mix. Smooth out the top of the dough.
3. Using the spatula and then select bake, start and bake for about 50 minutes. After 50 minutes, insert a toothpick into the top center to test doneness.
4. Test the loaf again. When the bread is completely baked, remove the pan from the machine and let the bread

remain in the pan for10 minutes. Remove bread and cool in wire rack.

Nutrition:

Calories: 310 calories

Total Carbohydrate: 40 g

Fat: 13 g

Protein: 3 g

Blueberry Bread

Preparation Time: 3 hours 15 minutes

Cooking time: 40- 45 minutes

Servings: 1 loaf

Ingredients:

- 1⅛ to 1¼ cups Water
- 6 ounces Cream cheese, softened
- 2 tablespoons Butter or margarine
- ¼ cup Sugar
- 2 teaspoons Salt
- 4½ cups Bread flour
- 1½ teaspoons Grated lemon peel
- 2 teaspoons Cardamom
- 2 tablespoons Nonfat dry milk
- 2½ teaspoons Red star brand active dry yeast
- ⅔ cup d ried blueberries

Directions:

1. Place all Ingredients except dried blueberries in bread pan, using the least amount of liquid listed in the recipe. Select light crust setting and raisin/nut cycle. Press start.

2. Observe the dough as it kneads. After 5 to 10 minutes, if it appears dry and stiff or if your ma- chine sounds as if it's straining to knead it, add more liquid 1 tablespoon at

a time until dough forms a smooth, soft, pliable ball that is slightly tacky to the touch.

3. At the beep, add the dried blueberries.
4. After the baking cycle ends, remove bread from pan, place on cake rack, and allow to cool 1 hour before slicing.

Nutrition:

Calories: 180 calories

Total Carbohydrate: 250 g

Fat: 3 g

Protein: 9 g

Orange and Walnut Bread

Preparation Time: 2 hours 50 minutes

Cooking time: 45 minutes

Servings: 10- 15

Ingredients:

- 1 egg white
- 1 tablespoon water
- ½ cup warm whey
- 1 tablespoons yeast
- 4 tablespoons sugar
- 2 oranges, crushed
- 4 cups flour
- 1 teaspoon salt
- 1 and ½ tablespoon salt
- 3 teaspoons orange peel
- 1/3 teaspoon vanilla
- 3 tablespoons walnut and almonds, crushed
- Crushed pepper, salt, cheese for garnish

Directions:

1. Add all of the ingredients to your Bread Machine (except egg white, 1 tablespoon water and crushed pepper/ cheese).

2. Set the program to "Dough" cycle and let the cycle run.

3. Remove the dough (using lightly floured hands) and carefully place it on a floured surface.

4. Cover with a light film/cling paper and let the dough rise for 10 minutes.

5. Divide the dough into thirds after it has risen

6. Place on a lightly flour surface, roll each portion into 14x10 inch sized rectangles

7. Use a sharp knife to cut carefully cut the dough into strips of ½ inch width

8. Pick 2-3 strips and twist them multiple times, making sure to press the ends together

9. Preheat your oven to 400 degrees F

10. Take a bowl and stir egg white, water and brush onto the breadsticks

11. Sprinkle salt, pepper/ cheese

12. Bake for 10-12 minutes until golden brown

13. Remove from baking sheet and transfer to cooling rack Serve and enjoy!

Nutrition:

Calories: 437 calories

Total Carbohydrate: 82 g

Total Fat: 7 g

Protein: 12 g

Sugar: 34 g

Fiber: 1 g

Sweet Breads

Brownie Bread

Preparation Time: 1 hour 15 minutes

Cooking time: 50 minutes

Servings: 1 loaf

Ingredients:

- 1 egg
- 1 egg yolk
- 1 teaspoon Salt
- 1/2 cup boiling water
- 1/2 cup cocoa powder, unsweetened
- 1/2 cup warm water
- 2 1/2 teaspoon Active dry yeast
- 2 tablespoon Vegetable oil
- 2 teaspoon White sugar
- 2/3 cup white sugar
- 3 cups bread flour

Directions:

1. Put the cocoa powder in a small bow. Pour boiling water and dissolve the cocoa powder.
2. Put the warm water, yeast and the 2 teaspoon White sugar in another bowl. Dissolve yeast and sugar. Let stand for about 10 minutes, or until the mix is creamy.

3. Place the cocoa mix, the yeast mix, the flour, the 2/3 cup white sugar, the salt, the vegetable, and the egg in the bread pan. Select basic bread cycle. Press start.

Nutrition:

Calories: 70 Cal

Fat: 3 g

Carbohydrates: 10 g

Protein: 1 g

Black Forest Bread

Preparation Time: 2 hour 15 minutes

Cooking time: 50 minutes

Servings: 1 loaf

Ingredients:

- 1 1/8 cups Warm water
- 1/3 cup Molasses
- 1 1/2 tablespoons Canola oil
- 1 1/2 cups Bread flour
- 1 cup Rye flour
- 1 cup Whole wheat flour
- 1 1/2 teaspoons Salt
- 3 tablespoons Cocoa powder
- 1 1/2 tablespoons Caraway seeds
- 2 teaspoons Active dry yeast

Directions:

1. Place all ingredients into your bread maker according to manufacture.
2. Select type to a light crust.
3. Press start.
4. Remembering to check while starting to knead.
5. If mixture is too dry add tablespoon warm water at a time.
6. If mixture is too wet add flour again a little at a time.

7. Mixture should go into a ball form, and just soft and slightly sticky to the finger touch. This goes for all types of breads when kneading.

Nutrition:

Calories: 240 Cal

Fat: 4 g

Carbohydrates: 29 g

Protein: 22 g

Sweet Almond Anise Bread

Preparation Time: 2 hours 20 minutes

Cooking time: 50 minutes

Servings: 1 loaf

Ingredients:

- ¾ cup water
- ¼ cup butter
- ¼ cup sugar
- ½ teaspoon salt
- 3 cups bread flour
- 1 teaspoon anise seed
- 2 teaspoons active dry yeast
- ½ cup almonds, chopped

Directions:

1. Add all of the ingredients to your bread machine, carefully following the instructions of the manufacturer
2. Set the program of your bread machine to Basic/White Bread and set crust type to Medium
3. Press START
4. Wait until the cycle completes
5. Once the loaf is ready, take the bucket out and let the loaf cool for 5 minutes
6. Gently shake the bucket to remove the loaf
7. Transfer to a cooling rack, slice and serve
   Enjoy!

Nutrition:

Calories: 87 Cal

Fat: 4 g

Carbohydrates: 7 g

Protein: 3 g

Fiber: 1 g

Chocolate Ginger and Hazelnut Bread

Preparation Time: 2 hours 50 minutes

Cooking time: 45 minutes

Servings: 2 loaves

Ingredients:

- 1/2 cup chopped hazelnuts
- 2 teaspoon bread machine yeast
- 3 1/2 cups bread flour
- 1 teaspoon salt
- 1 1/2 tablespoon dry skim milk powder
- 3 tablespoon light brown sugar
- 2 tablespoon candied ginger, chopped
- 1/3 cup unsweetened coconut
- 1 1/2 tablespoon unsalted butter, cubed
- 1 cup, plus 2 tablespoon water, with a temperature of 80 to 90 degrees F (26 to 32 degrees C)

Directions:

1. Put all the ingredients, except the hazelnuts, in the pan in this order: water, butter, coconut, candied ginger, brown sugar, milk, salt, flour, and yeast.
2. Secure the pan in the machine and close the lid. Put the toasted hazelnuts in the fruit and nut dispenser.
3. Turn the machine on. Select the basic setting and your desired color of the crust and press start.

4. Once done, carefully transfer the baked bread to a wire rack until cooled.

Nutrition:

Calories: 273 calories

Total Carbohydrate: 43 g

Total Fat: 11 g

Protein: 7 g

White Chocolate Bread

Preparation Time: 3 hours

Cooking time: 15 minutes

Servings: 12

Ingredients:

- 1/4 cup warm water
- 1 cup warm milk
- 1 egg
- 1/4 cup butter, softened
- 3 cups bread flour
- 2 tablespoons brown sugar
- 2 tablespoons white sugar
- 1 teaspoon salt
- 1 teaspoon ground cinnamon
- 1 (.25 oz.) package active dry yeast
- 1 cup white chocolate chips

Directions:

1. Put all the ingredients together, except for the white chocolate chips, into the bread machine pan following the order suggested by the manufacturer.
2. Choose the cycle on the machine and press the Start button to run the machine.
3. Put in the white chocolate chips at the machine's signal if the machine used has a Fruit setting on it or you may

put the white chocolate chips about 5 minutes before the kneading cycle ends.

Nutrition:

Calories: 277 calories

Total Carbohydrate: 39 g

Cholesterol: 30 mg

Total Fat: 10.5 g

Protein: 6.6 g

Sodium: 253 mg

Cinnamon Raisin Bread

Preparation Time: 5 minutes

Cooking time: 3 hours

Servings: 1 loaf

Ingredients:

- 1 cup water
- 2 tablespoons margarine
- 3 cups flour
- 3 tablespoons sugar
- 1 1/2 teaspoons salt
- 1 teaspoon cinnamon
- 2 1/2 teaspoons yeast
- 3/4 cup raisins

Directions:

1. Add all the ingredients into pan except raisins.
2. Choose sweet bread setting.
3. When the machine beeps, add in raisins.

Nutrition:

Calories: 141 calories

Total Carbohydrate: 26 g

Cholesterol: 00 mg

Total Fat: 2 g

Protein: 3.5 g

Sodium: 329 mg

Fiber: 1 g

Vegetable Breads

Healthy Celery Loaf

Preparation Time: 2 hours 40 minutes

Cooking time: 50 minutes

Servings: 1 loaf

Ingredients:

- 1 can (10 ounces) cream of celery soup
- 3 tablespoons low-fat milk, heated
- 1 tablespoon vegetable oil
- 1¼ teaspoons celery salt
- ¾ cup celery, fresh/sliced thin
- 1 tablespoon celery leaves, fresh, chopped
- 1 whole egg
- ¼ teaspoon sugar
- 3 cups bread flour
- ¼ teaspoon ginger
- ½ cup quick-cooking oats
- 2 tablespoons gluten
- 2 teaspoons celery seeds
- 1 pack of active dry yeast

Directions:

1. Add all of the ingredients to your bread machine, carefully following the instructions of the manufacturer
2. Set the program of your bread machine to Basic/White Bread and set crust type to Medium

3. Press START
4. Wait until the cycle completes
5. Once the loaf is ready, take the bucket out and let the loaf cool for 5 minutes
6. Gently shake the bucket to remove the loaf
7. Transfer to a cooling rack, slice and serve

   Enjoy!

Nutrition:

Calories: 73 Cal

Fat: 4 g

Carbohydrates:8 g

Protein: 3 g

Fiber: 1 g

Broccoli and Cauliflower Bread

Preparation Time: 2 hours 20 minutes

Cooking time: 50 minutes

Servings: 1 loaf

Ingredients:

- ¼ cup water
- 4 tablespoons olive oil
- 1 egg white
- 1 teaspoon lemon juice
- 2/3 cup grated cheddar cheese
- 3 tablespoons green onion
- ½ cup broccoli, chopped
- ½ cup cauliflower, chopped
- ½ teaspoon lemon pepper seasoning
- 2 cups bread flour
- 1 teaspoon bread machine yeast

Directions:

1. Add all of the ingredients to your bread machine, carefully following the instructions of the manufacturer
2. Set the program of your bread machine to Basic/White Bread and set crust type to Medium
3. Press START
4. Wait until the cycle completes

5. Once the loaf is ready, take the bucket out and let the loaf cool for 5 minutes
6. Gently shake the bucket to remove the loaf
7. Transfer to a cooling rack, slice and serve

   Enjoy!

Nutrition:

Calories: 156 Cal

Fat: 8 g

Carbohydrates: 17 g

Protein: 5 g

Fiber: 2 g

Zucchini Herbed Bread

Preparation Time: 2 hours 20 minutes

Cooking time: 50 minutes

Servings: 1 loaf

Ingredients:

- ½ cup water
- 2 teaspoon honey
- 1 tablespoons oil
- ¾ cup zucchini, grated
- ¾ cup whole wheat flour
- 2 cups bread flour
- 1 tablespoon fresh basil, chopped
- 2 teaspoon sesame seeds
- 1 teaspoon salt
- 1½ teaspoon active dry yeast

Directions:

1. Add all of the ingredients to your bread machine, carefully following the instructions of the manufacturer
2. Set the program of your bread machine to Basic/White Bread and set crust type to Medium
3. Press START
4. Wait until the cycle completes
5. Once the loaf is ready, take the bucket out and let the loaf cool for 5 minutes
6. Gently shake the bucket to remove the loaf

7. Transfer to a cooling rack, slice and serve Enjoy!

Nutrition:

Calories: 153 Cal

Fat: 1 g

Carbohydrates: 28 g

Protein: 5 g

Fiber: 2 g

Sourdough Breads

Sourdough Starter

Preparation Time: 5 days

Cooking time:

Servings:

Ingredients:

- 2 cups warm water
- 1 tablespoon sugar
- 1 active dry yeast
- 2 cups flour
- 1 proper container
- 1 spoon for stirring

Directions:

Day 1:

Combine the water, yeast, and sugar in a medium bowl, and whisk to combine. Gently stir in the flour until well combined, and transfer to your container. Let it sit, loosely covered, in a warm spot for 24 hours.

Day 2 - 4

Unlike the traditional starter, you don't need to feed this one yet. Stir it once or twice every 24 hours.

Day 5:

By now the starter should have developed the classic slightly sour smell. If not, don't worry; you just need to let it sit a bit longer. If it is ready, store it in the fridge, and feed it once a week until you're ready to use it. As with the traditional starter, you'll need to feed it the day before you plan to use it.

Nutrition:

Calories: 26 Cal

Fat: 0 g

Carbohydrates: 6 g

Protein: 1 g

Garlic and Herb Flatbread Sourdough

Preparation Time: 1 hour

Cooking time: 25- 30 minutes

Servings: 12

Ingredients:

- Dough
- 1 cup sourdough starter, fed or unfed
- 3/4 cup warm water
- 2 teaspoons instant yeast
- 3 cups all-purpose flour
- 1 1/2 teaspoons salt
- 3 tablespoons olive oil
- Topping
- 1/2 teaspoon dried thyme
- 1/2 teaspoon dried oregano
- 1/2 teaspoon dried marjoram
- 1 teaspoon garlic powder
- 1/4 teaspoon onion powder
- 1/4 teaspoon salt
- 1/4 teaspoon pepper
- 3 tablespoons olive oil

Directions:

1. Combine all the dough ingredients in the bowl of a stand mixer, and knead until smooth. Place in a lightly

greased bowl and let rise for at least one hour. Punch down, then let rise again for at least one hour.

2. To prepare the topping, mix all ingredients except the olive oil in a small bowl.

3. Lightly grease a 9x13 baking pan or standard baking sheet, and pat and roll the dough into a long rectangle in the pan. Brush the olive oil over the dough, and sprinkle the herb and seasoning mixture over top. Cover and let rise for 15-20 minutes.

4. Preheat oven to 425F and bake for 25-30 minutes.

Nutrition:

Calories: 89 Cal

Fat: 3.7 g

Protein: 1.8 g

Dinner Rolls

Preparation Time: 3 hours

Cooking time: 5-10 minutes

Servings: 24 rolls

Ingredients:

- 1 cup sourdough starter
- 1 1/2 cups warm water
- 1 tablespoon yeast
- 1 tablespoon salt
- 2 tablespoons sugar
- 2 tablespoons olive oil
- 5 cups all-purpose flour
- 2 tablespoons butter, melted

Directions:

1. In a large bowl, mix the sourdough starter, water, yeast, salt, sugar, and oil. Add the flour, stirring until the mixture forms a dough. If needed, add more flour. Place the dough in a greased bowl, and let it rise until doubled in size, about 2 hours.

2. Remove the dough from the bowl, and divide it into 2-3 inch sized pieces. Place the buns into a greased 9x13 pan, and let them rise, covered, for about an hour.

3. Preheat oven to 350F, and bake the rolls for 15 minutes. Remove from the oven, brush with the melted butter, and bake for an additional 5-10 minutes.

Nutrition:

Calories: 128 Cal

Fat: 2.4 g

Protein: 3.2 g

Sugar: 1.1 g

Sourdough Boule

Preparation Time: 4 hours

Cooking time: 25-35 minutes

Servings: 12

Ingredients:

- 275g Warm Water
- 500g sourdough starter
- 550g all-purpose flour
- 20g Salt

Directions:

1. Combine the flour, warm water, and starter, and let sit, covered for at least 30 minutes.

2. After letting it sit, stir in the salt, and turn the dough out onto a floured surface. It will be quite sticky, but that's okay. Flatten the dough slightly (it's best to "slap" it onto the counter), then fold it in half a few times.

3. Cover the dough and let it rise. Repeat the slap and fold a few more times. Now cover the dough and let it rise for 2-4 hours.

4. When the dough at least doubles in size, gently pull it so the top of the dough is taught. Repeat several times. Let it rise for 2-4 hours once more.

5. Preheat to oven to 475F, and either place a baking stone or a cast iron pan in the oven to preheat. Place the risen dough on the stone or pot, and score the top in several

spots. Bake for 20 minutes, then lower the heat to 425F, and bake for 25-35 minutes more. The boule will be golden brown.

Nutrition:

Calories: 243 Cal

Fat: 0.7 g

Protein: 6.9 g

Holiday Bread

Pumpkin Bread

Preparation time: 5 minutes

Cooking time: 1 hour

Servings: 14

Ingredients:

- ½ cup plus 2 tablespoons warm water
- ½ cup canned pumpkin puree
- ¼ cup butter, softened
- ¼ cup non-fat dry milk powder
- 2¾ cups bread flour
- ¼ cup brown sugar
- ¾ teaspoon salt
- 1 teaspoon ground cinnamon
- ½ teaspoon ground ginger
- 1/8 teaspoon ground nutmeg
- 2¼ teaspoons active dry yeast

Directions:

1. Place all ingredients in the baking pan of the bread machine in the order recommended by the manufacturer.
2. Place the baking pan in the bread machine and close the lid.
3. Select Basic setting.
4. Press the start button.

5. Carefully, remove the baking pan from the machine and then invert the bread loaf onto a wire rack to cool completely before slicing.
6. With a sharp knife, cut bread loaf into desired-sized slices and serve.

Nutrition:

Calories: 134

Total Fat: 3.6 g

Saturated Fat: 2.1 g

Cholesterol: 9 mg

Sodium: 149 mg

Total Carbs: 22.4 g

Fiber: 1.1 g

Sugar: 2.9 g

Protein: 2.9 g

Pumpkin Cranberry Bread

Preparation time: 10 minutes

Cooking time: 4 hours

Servings: 12

Ingredients:

- ¾ cup water
- 2/3 cup canned pumpkin
- 3 tablespoons brown sugar
- 2 tablespoons vegetable oil
- 2 cups all-purpose flour
- 1 cup whole-wheat flour
- 1¼ teaspoon salt
- ½ cup sweetened dried cranberries
- ½ cup walnuts, chopped
- 1¾ teaspoons active dry yeast

Directions:

1. Place all ingredients in the baking pan of the bread machine in the order recommended by the manufacturer.
2. Place the baking pan in the bread machine and close the lid.
3. Select Basic setting.
4. Press the start button.

5. Carefully, remove the baking pan from the machine and then invert the bread loaf onto a wire rack to cool completely before slicing.
6. With a sharp knife, cut bread loaf into desired-sized slices and serve.

Nutrition:

Calories: 199

Total Fat: 6 g

Saturated Fat: 0.7 g

Cholesterol: 0 mg

Sodium: 247 mg

Total Carbs: 31.4 g

Fiber: 3.2 g

Sugar: 5.1 g

Protein: 5.6 g

Cheese Breads

Cheddar Cheese Basil Bread

Preparation Time: 10 Minutes

Cooking Time: 25 Minutes

Servings: 8

Ingredients:

- 1 cup milk
- One tablespoon melted butter cooled
- One tablespoon sugar
- One teaspoon dried basil
- ¾ cup (3 ounces) shredded sharp Cheddar cheese
- ¾ teaspoon salt
- 3 cups white bread flour
- 1½ teaspoons active dry yeast

Directions:

1. Preparing the Ingredients. Place the ingredients in your Zojirushi bread machine.
2. Select the Bake cycle. Program the machine for Regular Basic, choose light or medium crust, and then press Start.
3. If the loaf is done, remove the bucket from the machine.
4. Let the loaf cool for 5 minutes.
5. Softly shake the canister to remove the loaf and put it out onto a rack to cool.

Nutrition:

Calories: 174

Carbs: 31.1g

Fat: 3.1g

Protein: 5.1g

Herb and Parmesan Cheese Loaf

Preparation Time: 10 Minutes

Cooking Time: 25 Minutes

Servings: 8

Ingredients:

- 3 cups + 2 tbsp. all-purpose flour
- 1 cup of water
- 2 tbsp. oil
- 2 tbsp. sugar
- 3 tbsp. milk
- 1 tbsp. instant yeast
- 1 tsp. garlic powder
- 5 tbsp. parmesan cheese
- 1 tbsp. fresh basil
- 1 tbsp. fresh oregano
- 1 tbsp. fresh chives or rosemary

Directions:

1. Preparing the Ingredients. Place all fixings in the bread pan in the liquid-cheese and herb-dry-yeast layering.
2. Put the pan in the Zojirushi bread machine.
3. Select the Bake cycle. Choose Regular Basic Setting.
4. Press start and wait until the loaf is cooked.
5. The machine will start the keep warm mode after the bread is complete.

6. Just allow it to stay in that mode for about 10 minutes before unplugging.
7. Remove the pan and wait for it to cool down for about 10 minutes.

Nutrition:

Calories: 174

Carbs: 31.1 g

Fat: 3.1g

Protein: 5.1 g

Olive Cheese Bread

Preparation Time: 10 Minutes

Cooking Time: 25 Minutes

Servings: 8

Ingredients:

- 1 cup milk
- 1½ tablespoons melted butter, cooled
- One teaspoon minced garlic
- 1½ tablespoons sugar
- One teaspoon salt
- 3 cups white bread flour
- ¾ cup (3 ounces) shredded Swiss cheese
- One teaspoon bread machine or instant yeast
- 1/3 cup chopped black olives

Directions:

1. Preparing the Ingredients. Place the ingredients in your Zojirushi bread machine, tossing the flour with the cheese first.
2. Program the machine for Regular Basic, choose light or medium crust, and press Start.
3. Next, when the loaf is done, you may remove the bucket from the machine.
4. Let the loaf cool for 5 minutes.
5. Mildly shake the pot to eliminate the loaf and turn it out onto a rack to cool.

Nutrition:

Calories 174

Carbs 31.1g

Fat 3.1g

Protein 5.1g

Beer and Cheese Bread

Preparation Time: 10 Minutes

Cooking Time: 25 Minutes

Servings: 8

Ingredients:

- 3 cups bread or all-purpose flour

- 1 tbsp. instant yeast

- 1 tsp. salt

- 1 tbsp. sugar

- 1 1/2 cup beer at room temperature

- 1/2 cup shredded Monterey cheese

- 1/2 cup shredded Edam cheese

Directions:

1. Place all elements, except cheeses, in the bread pan in the liquid-dry-yeast layering.

2. Put the pan in the Zojirushi bread machine.

3. Select the Bake cycle. Choose Regular Basic Setting. Press Start.

4. When the kneading process is about to end, add the cheese.

5. Wait until the loaf is cooked.

6. The machine will start the keep warm mode after the bread is complete.

7. Do not forget to let it stay in that mode for about 10 minutes before unplugging.

8. Lastly, remove the pan and let it cool down for about 10 minutes.

Nutrition:

Calories 174

Carbs 31.1g

Fat 3.1g

Protein 5.1g

Blue Cheese Onion Bread

Preparation Time: 10 Minutes

Cooking Time: 25 Minutes

Servings: 8

Ingredients:

- 1¼ cup water, at 80°F to 90°F

- One egg, at room temperature

- One tablespoon melted butter cooled

- ¼ cup powdered skim milk

- One tablespoon sugar

- ¾ teaspoon salt

- ½ cup (2 ounces) crumbled blue cheese

- One tablespoon dried onion flake

- 3 cups white bread flour

- ¼ cup instant mashed potato flakes

- One teaspoon bread machine or active dry yeast

Directions:

1. Preparing the Ingredients. Place the ingredients in your Zojirushi bread machine.

2. Program the machine for Regular Basic, select light or medium crust, and press Start.

3. Remove the bucket from the machine.

4. Let the loaf cool for 5 minutes.

5. Gently shake the container to remove the loaf and turn it out onto a rack to cool.

Nutrition:

Calories 174

Carbs 31.1g

Fat 3.1g

Protein 5.1g

Nut and Seed Breads

Flax and Sunflower Seed Bread

Preparation Time: 5 Minutes

Cooking Time: 25 Minutes

Servings: 8

Ingredients:

- 1 1/3 cups water
- Two tablespoons butter softened
- Three tablespoons honey
- 2/3 cups of bread flour
- One teaspoon salt
- One teaspoon active dry yeast
- 1/2 cup flax seeds
- 1/2 cup sunflower seeds

Directions:

1. With the manufacturer's suggested order, add all the ingredients (apart from sunflower seeds) to the bread machine's pan.
2. The select basic white cycle, then press start.
3. Just in the knead cycle that your machine signals alert sounds, add the sunflower seeds.

Nutrition:

Calories: 140 calories;

Sodium: 169

Total Carbohydrate: 22.7

Cholesterol: 4
Protein: 4.2
Total Fat: 4.2

Honey and Flaxseed Bread

Preparation Time: 5 Minutes

Cooking Time: 25 Minutes

Servings: 8

Ingredients:

- 1 1/8 cups water
- 1 1/2 tablespoons flaxseed oil
- Three tablespoons honey
- 1/2 tablespoon liquid lecithin
- 3 cups whole wheat flour
- 1/2 cup flax seed
- Two tablespoons bread flour
- Three tablespoons whey powder
- 1 1/2 teaspoons sea salt
- Two teaspoons active dry yeast

Directions:

1. In the bread machine pan, put in all of the ingredients following the order recommended by the manufacturer.
2. Choose the Wheat cycle on the machine and press the Start button to run the machine.

Nutrition:

Calories: 174 calories

Protein: 7.1

Total Fat: 4.9

Sodium: 242

Total Carbohydrate: 30.8

Cholesterol: 1

Pumpkin and Sunflower Seed Bread

Preparation Time: 5 Minutes

Cooking Time: 25 Minutes

Servings: 8

Ingredients:

- 1 (.25 ounce) package instant yeast
- 1 cup of warm water
- 1/4 cup honey
- Four teaspoons vegetable oil
- 3 cups whole wheat flour
- 1/4 cup wheat bran (optional)
- One teaspoon salt
- 1/3 cup sunflower seeds
- 1/3 cup shelled, toasted, chopped pumpkin seeds

Directions:

1. Into the bread machine, put the ingredients according to the order suggested by the manufacturer.
2. Next is setting the machine to the whole wheat setting, then press the start button.
3. You can add the pumpkin and sunflower seeds at the beep if your bread machine has a signal for nuts or fruit.

Nutrition:

Calories: 148 calories

Total Carbohydrate: 24.1

Cholesterol: 0

Protein: 5.1

Total Fat: 4.8

Sodium: 158

Seven Grain Bread

Preparation Time: 5 Minutes

Cooking Time: 25 Minutes

Servings: 8

Ingredients:

- 1 1/3 cups warm water
- One tablespoon active dry yeast
- Three tablespoons dry milk powder
- Two tablespoons vegetable oil
- Two tablespoons honey
- Two teaspoons salt
- One egg
- 1 cup whole wheat flour
- 2 1/2 cups bread flour
- 3/4 cup 7-grain cereal

Directions:

1. Follow the order of putting the ingredients into the pan of the bread machine recommended by the manufacturer.
2. Choose the Whole Wheat Bread cycle on the machine and press the Start button to run the machine.

Nutrition:

Calories: 285 calories

Total Fat: 5.2

Sodium: 629

Total Carbohydrate: 50.6

Cholesterol: 24

Protein: 9.8

Wheat Bread with Flax Seed

Preparation Time: 5 Minutes

Cooking Time: 25 Minutes

Servings: 8

Ingredients:

- 1 (.25 ounce) package active dry yeast
- 1 1/4 cups whole wheat flour
- 3/4 cup ground flax seed
- 1 cup bread flour
- One tablespoon vital wheat gluten
- Two tablespoons dry milk powder
- One teaspoon salt
- 1 1/2 tablespoons vegetable oil
- 1/4 cup honey
- 1 1/2 cups water

Directions:

1. In the bread machine pan, put the ingredients following the order recommendation of the manufacturer.
2. Make sure to select the cycle and then press Start.

Nutrition:

Calories: 168 calories

Total Carbohydrate: 22.5

Cholesterol: 1

Protein: 5.5
Total Fat: 7.3
Sodium: 245

Spice and Herb Breads

Italian Herb Bread

Preparation Time: 5 Minutes

Cooking Time: 3 Hours and 5 Minutes

Servings: 14 slices

Ingredients:

- 2 Tbsp margarine
- 2 Tbsp sugar
- 1½ cups water
- 3 Tbsp powdered milk
- 1½ tsp. dried marjoram
- 1½ tsp. dried basil
- 1½ tsp. salt
- 4 cups bread flour
- 1¼ tsp. yeast
- 1½ tsp. dried thyme

Directions:

1. Add each ingredient to the bread machine in the instruction and at the temperature recommended by your bread machine manufacturer.
2. Close the lid, choose the basic bread, medium crust setting on your bread machine, then press start.
3. If the bread machine has finished baking, remove the bread.
4. Put it on a cooling rack.

Nutrition:

Carbs: 20 g

Fat: 3 g

Protein: 4 g

Calories: 120

Caramelized Onion Bread

Preparation Time: 15 Minutes

Cooking Time: 3 Hours and 35 Minutes

Servings: 14 slices

Ingredients:

- ½ Tbsp butter
- ½ cup onions, sliced
- 1 cup of water
- 1 Tbsp olive oil
- 3 cups Gold Medal Better
- 1 tsp. salt
- 1¼ tsp. quick active dry yeast

Directions:

1. Melt the butter through medium-low heat in a skillet.
2. Cook the onions in the butter for 10 to 15 minutes until they are brown and caramelized - then remove from the heat.
3. Add each ingredient except the onions to the bread machine.
4. Select the basic bread, medium crust setting on your bread machine, and press start.
5. Add ½ cup of onions 5 to 10 minutes before the last kneading cycle ends.
6. When the bread machine has ended baking, remove the bread and put it on a cooling rack.

Nutrition:

Carbs: 30 g

Fat: 3 g

Protein: 4 g

Calories: 160

Olive Bread

Preparation Time: 10 Minutes

Cooking Time: 3 Hours

Servings: 14 slices

Ingredients:

- ½ cup brine from the olive jar
- Add warm water (110°F) To make 1½ cup when combined with brine
- 2 Tbsp olive oil
- 3 cups bread flour
- 1 2/3 cups whole wheat flour
- 1 ½ tsp. salt
- 2 Tbsp sugar
- 1 1/2 tsp. dried leaf basil
- 2 tsp. active dry yeast
- 2/3 cup finely chopped Kalamata olives

Directions:

1. Add each ingredient except the olives to the bread machine.
2. Close the lid, select the wheat, medium crust setting on your bread machine, and press start.
3. Add the olives 10 minutes before the last kneading cycle ends.
4. When the bread machine has finished baking, get the bread and put it on a cooling rack.

Nutrition:

Carbs: 28 g

Fat: 1 g

Protein: 5 g

Calories: 140

Keto Bread

Simple Bread

Preparation Time: 3 minutes

Cooking time: 3 minutes

Servings: 8

Ingredients:

- 3 cups almond flour
- 2 tbsp inulin
- 1 tbsp whole milk
- ½ tsp salt
- 2 tsp active yeast
- 1 ¼ cups warm water
- 1 tbsp olive oil

Directions:

1. Use a small mixing bowl to combine all dry Ingredients, except for the yeast.
2. In the bread machine pan add all wet Ingredients.
3. Add all of your dry Ingredients, from the small mixing bowl, in the bread machine pan. Top with the yeast.
4. Set the bread machine to the basic bread setting.
5. When the bread is done, remove bread machine pan from the bread machine.
6. Let cool slightly before transferring to a cooling rack.
7. The bread can be stored for up to 5 days on the counter and for up to 3 months in the freezer.

Nutrition:

Carbohydrates: 4 g

Fats: 7 g

Protein: 3 g

Calories: 85

Fiber: 1.5 g

Toast Bread

Preparation Time: 3 ½ hours

Cooking time: 3 ½ hours

Servings: 8

Ingredients:

- 1 ½ teaspoons yeast
- 3 cups almond flour
- 2 tablespoons sugar
- 1 teaspoon salt
- 1 ½ tablespoons butter
- 1 cup water

Directions:

1. Pour water into the bowl; add salt, sugar, soft butter, flour, and yeast.
2. I add dried tomatoes and paprika.
3. Put it on the basic program.
4. The crust can be light or medium.

Nutrition: Carbohydrates: 5 g

Fats: 2.7 g

Protein: 5.2 g

Calories: 203

Fiber: 1 g

Keto Bakers Bread

Preparation Time: 10 minutes

Cooking time: 20 minutes

Servings: 12

Ingredients:

- Pinch of salt
- 4 tbsp. light cream cheese softened
- ½ tsp. cream of tartar
- 4 eggs, yolks, and whites separated

Directions:

1. Heat 2 racks in the middle of the oven at 350F.
2. Line 2 baking pan with parchment paper, then grease with cooking spray.
3. Separate egg yolks from the whites and place them in separate mixing bowls.
4. Beat the egg whites and cream of tartar with a hand mixer until stiff, about 3 to 5 minutes. Do not over-beat.
5. Whisk the cream cheese, salt, and egg yolks until smooth.
6. Slowly fold the cheese mix into the whites until fluffy.
7. Spoon ¼ cup measure of the batter onto the baking sheets, 6 mounds on each sheet.
8. Bake in the oven for 20 to 22 minutes, alternating racks halfway through.
9. Cool and serve.

Nutrition:

Calories: 41

Fat: 3.2 g

Carb: 1 g

Protein: 2.4 g

Walnut Bread

Preparation Time: 4 hours

Cooking time: 4 hours

Servings: 10

Ingredients:

- 4 cups almond flour
- ½ cup water
- ½ cup milk
- 2 eggs
- ½ cup walnuts
- 1 tablespoon vegetable oil
- 1 tablespoon sugar
- 1 teaspoon salt
- 1 teaspoon yeast

Directions:

1. All products must be room temperature.
2. Pour water, milk, and vegetable oil into the bucket and add in the eggs.
3. Now pour in the sifted almond flour. In the process of kneading bread, you may need a little more or less flour – it depends on its moisture.
4. Pour in salt, sugar, and yeast. If it is hot in the kitchen (especially in summer), pour all three Ingredients into the different ends of the bucket so that the dough does not have time for peroxide.

5. Now the first kneading dough begins, which lasts 15 minutes. In the process, we monitor the state of the ball. It should be soft, but at the same time, keep its shape and not spread. If the ball does not want to be collected, add a little flour, since the moisture of this product is different for everyone. If the bucket is clean and all the flour is incorporated into the dough, then everything is done right. If the dough is still lumpy and even crumbles, you need to add a little more liquid.

6. Close the lid and then prepare the nuts. They need to be sorted and lightly fried in a dry frying pan; the pieces of nuts will be crispy. Then let them cool and cut with a knife to the desired size. When the bread maker signals, pour in the nuts and wait until the spatula mixes them into the dough.

7. Remove the bucket and take out the walnut bread. Completely cool it on a grill so that the bottom does not get wet.

Nutrition:

Carbohydrates: 4 g

Fats: 6.7 g

Protein: 8.3 g

Calories: 257

Fiber: 1.3 g

Bulgur Bread

Preparation Time: 3 hours

Cooking time: 3 hours

Servings: 8

Ingredients:

- ½ cup bulgur
- 1/3 cup boiling water
- 1 egg
- 1 cup water
- 1 tablespoon butter
- 1 ½ tablespoon milk powder
- 1 tablespoon sugar
- 2 teaspoons salt
- 3 ¼ cup flour
- 1 teaspoon dried yeast

Directions:

1. Bulgur pour boiling water into a small container and cover with a lid. Leave to stand for 30 minutes.
2. Cut butter into small cubes.
3. Stir the egg with water in a measuring container. The total volume of eggs with water should be 300 ml.
4. Put all the Ingredients in the bread maker in the order that is described in the instructions for your bread maker. Bake in the basic mode, medium crust.

Nutrition:

Calories: 937 calories

Total Carbohydrate: 196 g

Total Fat: 0.4 g

Protein: 26.5 g

Sodium: 1172 mg

Fiber: 7.3 g

Italian Blue Cheese Bread

Preparation Time: 3 hours

Cooking time: 3 hours

Servings: 8

Ingredients:

- 1 teaspoon dry yeast
- 2 ½ cups almond flour
- 1 ½ teaspoon salt
- 1 tablespoon sugar
- 1 tablespoon olive oil
- ½ cup blue cheese
- 1 cup water

Directions:

Mix all the Ingredients. Start baking.

Nutrition:

Calories: 237 calories

Total Fat: 0.4 g

Protein: 26.5 g

Sodium: 1172 mg

Fiber: 7.3 g

Cream Cheese Bread

Preparation Time: 10 minutes

Cooking time: 4 hours

Serving: 1 ½ pounds / 12 slices

Ingredients:

- ¼ cup / 60 grams butter, grass-fed, unsalted
- 1 cup and 3 tablespoons / 140 grams cream cheese, softened
- 4 egg yolks, pasteurized
- 1 teaspoon vanilla extract, unsweetened
- 1 teaspoon baking powder
- ¼ teaspoon of sea salt
- 2 tablespoons monk fruit powder
- ½ cup / 65 grams peanut flour

Directions:

1. Gather all the ingredients for the bread and plug in the bread machine having the capacity of 2 pounds of bread recipe.

2. Take a large bowl, place butter in it, beat in cream cheese until thoroughly combined and then beat in egg yolks, vanilla, baking powder, salt, and monk fruit powder until well combined.

3. Add egg mixture into the bread bucket, top with flour, shut the lid, select the "basic/white" cycle or "low-carb" setting and then press the up/down arrow button to

adjust baking time according to your bread machine; it will take 3 to 4 hours.

4. Then press the crust button to select light crust if available, and press the "start/stop" button to switch on the bread machine.

5. When the bread machine beeps, open the lid, then take out the bread basket and lift out the bread.

6. Let bread cool on a wire rack for 1 hour, then cut it into twelve slices and serve.

Nutrition:

Calories: 347 calories

Protein: 26.5 g

Sodium: 1172 mg

Fiber: 7.3 g

Gluten free Bread

Pumpkin bread

Preparation Time: 5 minutes
Cooking time: 15 minutes
Serving: 8
Ingredients:

- 6 eggs
- 8 tbsp. butter, melted
- 2 cups almond flour
- 2 teaspoons baking powder
- ¼ teaspoon ground allspice
- ¼ teaspoon ground cloves
- ¼ teaspoon ground nutmeg
- ½ cup erythritol
- ½ cup pumpkin puree
- 1 tsp. cinnamon
- 3 tbsp. sour cream
- 1 teaspoon vanilla
- 2 tbsp. heavy cream

Directions:

1. In the bread machine pan add all the wet ingredients.
2. Then add the dry ingredients on top.
3. Set the bread machine to the gluten free bread setting.
4. When the bread is done, remove bread machine pan from the bread machine.

5. Let cool slightly before transferring to a cooling rack.

6. The bread can be stored for up to 5 days on the counter.

Nutrition:

Calories 220

Carbohydrates 14 g

Fats 21 g

Protein 6 g

Zucchini bread with walnuts

Preparation Time: 4 minutes

Cooking time: 15 minutes

Serving: 12

Ingredients:

- 2 ½ cups almond flour
- ½ cup olive oil
- 1.5 cups erythritol
- 1 tsp. vanilla extract
- ½ tsp. nutmeg
- 3 large eggs
- 1 ½ tsp. baking powder
- 1 cup grated zucchinis
- 1 tsp. cinnamon
- ¼ tsp. ginger
- ½ tsp. salt
- ½ cup walnuts, chopped

Directions:

1. Grate zucchini and use cheesecloth to squeeze excess water out and set aside.
2. Mix eggs, vanilla extract, and oil in bread machine pan.
3. Add almond flour, ginger, erythritol, salt, nutmeg, baking powder and cinnamon.

4. Add the zucchini to the bread machine pan and top with walnuts.
5. Set bread machine to gluten free.
6. When the bread is done, remove bread machine pan from the bread machine.
7. Let cool slightly before transferring to a cooling rack.
8. The bread can be stored for up to 5 days on the counter and for up to 3 months in the freezer.

Nutrition:

Calories 160

Carbohydrates 3 g

Fats 16 g

Protein 4 g

Greek Olive Bread

Preparation Time: 15 minutes

Cooking time: 15 minutes

Serving: 20

Ingredients:

- 4 eggs
- 5 tbsp. ground flaxseed
- 2 tsp. psyllium powder
- 2 tbsp. apple cider vinegar
- 1 tsp. baking soda
- 1 tsp. salt
- ½ cup sour cream
- ½ cup olive oil
- 1.8 oz. black olives, chopped
- 1 tsp. ground rosemary
- 1 ½ cup almond flour
- 1 tsp. dried basil

Directions:

1. Beat eggs in a mixing bowl for about 5 minutes. Add olive oil slowly while you continue to beat the eggs. Add in sour cream and apple cider vinegar and continue to beat for another 5 minutes.

2. Mix all of the remaining ingredients together in a separate smaller bowl.

3. Place all wet ingredients into bread machine pan.

4. Add the remaining ingredients to the bread pan.

5. Set bread machine to the French setting.

6. When the bread is done, remove bread machine pan from the bread machine.

7. Let cool slightly before transferring to a cooling rack.

8. The bread can be stored for up to 7 days on the counter.

Nutrition:

Calories: 150

Carbohydrates: 3g

Protein: 3g

Fat: 14g

Carrot Polenta Loaf

Preparation Time: 5 minutes

Cooking time: 3 hours

Servings: 1 loaf

Ingredients

- 10 oz. lukewarm water
- 2 tablespoons extra-virgin olive oil
- 1 tsp. salt
- 1 ½ tablespoons sugar
- 1 ½ tablespoons dried thyme
- 1 ½ cups freshly-grated carrots
- 1/2 cup yellow cornmeal
- 1 cup light rye flour
- 2 ½ cups bread flour
- 3 tsp. instant active dry yeast

Direction:

1. Add all ingredients to machine pan.
2. Select dough setting.
3. When cycle is complete, turn dough onto lightly floured surface
4. Knead the dough and shape into an oval; cover with plastic wrap and let rest for 10 to 15 minutes.
5. After resting, turn bottom side up and flatten.
6. Fold the top 1/3 of the way to the bottom. Then fold the bottom a 1/3 of the way over the top. Press dough with

palm of your hand to make an indent in the center, and then fold the top completely down to the bottom, sealing the seam.

7. Preheat oven 400.
8. Dust a baking sheet with cornmeal, place dough on and cover in a warm place to rise for 20 minutes.
9. After rising, make 3 deep diagonal slashes on the top and brush the top of the bread with cold water.
10. 10 Bake for 20 to 25 minutes or until nicely browned

Nutrition:

146 Calories,

2 g total fat (0 g sat. fat)

1 mg chol

186 mg sodium

27 g carb

2 fiber

3.9 g protein

Veggie Loaf

Preparation Time: 20 minutes

Cooking time: 15 minutes

Serving: 20

Ingredients:

- 1/3 cup coconut flour
- 2 tablespoons chia Seed
- 2 tbsp. psyllium husk powder
- ¼ cup sunflower seeds
- ¼ cup pumpkin seeds
- 2 tbsp. flax seed
- 1 cup almond flour
- 1 cup zucchini, grated
- 4 eggs
- ¼ cup coconut oil, melted
- 1 tbsp. paprika
- 2 tsp. cumin
- 2 tsp. baking powder
- 2 tsp. salt

Directions:

1. Grate carrots and zucchini; use cheesecloth to drain excess water, set aside.
2. Mix eggs and coconut oil into bread machine pan.
3. Add the remaining ingredients to bread pan.

4. Set bread machine to quick bread setting.

5. When the bread is done, remove bread machine pan from the bread machine.

6. Let cool slightly before transferring to a cooling rack.

7. You can store your veggie loaf bread for up to 5 days in the refrigerator, or you can also be sliced and stored in the freezer for up to 3 months.

Nutrition:

Calories: 150

Carbohydrates: 3g

Protein: 3g

Fat: 14g

Traditional Bread

Cauliflower Bread with Garlic & Herbs

Preparation Time: 9 minutes

Cooking time: 26 min

Serving: 12

Ingredients:

- 3 cup Cauliflower ("riced" utilizing nourishment processor*)
- 10 enormous Egg (isolated)
- 1/4 teaspoon Cream of tartar (discretionary)
- 1 1/4 cup Coconut flour
- 1 1/2 teaspoon sans gluten heating powder
- 1 teaspoon Sea salt
- 6 teaspoon Butter (unsalted, estimated strong, at that point softened; can utilize ghee for sans dairy)
- 6 cloves Garlic (minced)
- 1 teaspoon Fresh rosemary (slashed)
- 1 teaspoon Fresh parsley (slashed)

Direction:

1. Preheat the broiler to 350 degrees F (177 degrees C). Line a 9x5 in (23x13 cm) portion skillet with material paper.

2. Steam the riced cauliflower. You can do this in the microwave (cooked for 3-4 minutes, shrouded in plastic) OR in a steamer bin over water on the stove (line with cheesecloth if the openings in the steamer

container are too huge, and steam for a couple of moments). The two different ways, steam until the cauliflower is delicate and delicate. Enable the cauliflower to sufficiently cool to deal with.

3. Meanwhile, utilize a hand blender to beat the egg whites and cream of tartar until solid pinnacles structure.

4. Place the coconut flour, preparing powder, ocean salt, egg yolks, dissolved margarine, garlic, and 1/4 of the whipped egg whites in a nourishment processor.

5. When the cauliflower has cooled enough to deal with, envelop it by kitchen towel and press a few times to discharge however much dampness as could reasonably be expected. (This is significant - the final product ought to be dry and bunch together.) Add the cauliflower to the nourishment processor. Procedure until all-around joined. (Blend will be thick and somewhat brittle.)

6. Add the rest of the egg whites to the nourishment processor. Overlay in only a bit, to make it simpler to process. Heartbeat a couple of times until simply consolidated. (Blend will be cushioned.) Fold in the hacked parsley and rosemary. (Don't over-blend to abstain from separating the egg whites excessively.)

7. Transfer the player into the lined heating skillet. Smooth the top and adjust somewhat. Whenever

wanted, you can squeeze more herbs into the top (discretionary).

8. Bake for around 45-50 minutes, until the top, is brilliant. Cool totally before expelling and cutting.

9. How To Make Buttered Low Carb Garlic Bread (discretionary): Top cuts liberally with spread, minced garlic, crisp parsley, and a little ocean salt. Prepare in a preheated stove at 450 degrees F (233 degrees C) for around 10 minutes. On the off chance that you need it progressively sautéed, place under the oven for several minutes.

Nutrition:

Cal: 70

Carbs: 4g

Net Carbs: 2.5 g

Fiber: 4.5 g

Fat: 15 g

Protein: 4g

Sugars: 3 g

Grain-Free Tortillas Bread

Preparation Time: 5 minutes

Cooking time: 20 min

Serving: 5

Ingredients:

- 96 g almond flour
- 24 g coconut flour
- 2 teaspoons thickener
- 1 teaspoon heating powder
- 1/4 teaspoon fit salt
- 2 teaspoons apple juice vinegar
- 1 egg softly beaten
- 3 teaspoons water

Directions:

1. Add almond flour, coconut flour, thickener, preparing powder and salt to nourishment processor. Heartbeat until wholly joined. Note: you can, on the other hand, whisk everything in a vast bowl and utilize a hand or stand blender for the accompanying advances.

2. Pour in apple juice vinegar with the nourishment processor running. When it has dispersed equally, pour in the egg. Pursued by the water, stop the nourishment processor once the batter structures into a ball. The batter will be clingy to contact.

3. Wrap mixture in stick film and ply it through the plastic for a moment or two. Consider it somewhat like a pressure ball. Enable the variety to rest for 10 minutes (and as long as three days in the refrigerator).

4. Heat up a skillet (ideally) or container over medium warmth. You can test the warmth by sprinkling a couple of water beads if the drops vanish promptly your dish are excessively hot. The beads should 'go' through the skillet.

5. Break the mixture into eight 1" balls (26g each). Turn out between two sheets of material or waxed paper with a moving pin or utilizing a tortilla press (simpler!) until each round is 5-crawls in distance across.

6. Transfer to skillet and cook over medium warmth for only 3-6 seconds (significant). Flip it over promptly (utilizing a meager spatula or blade), and keep on cooking until just daintily brilliant on each side (however with the customary roasted imprints), 30 to 40 seconds. The key isn't to overcook them, as they will never again be flexible or puff up.

7. Keep them warm enclosed by kitchen fabric until serving. To rewarm, heat quickly on the two sides, until simply warm (not exactly a moment)

8. These tortillas are best destroyed straight. Be that as it may, don't hesitate to keep some mixture convenient in

your ice chest for as long as three days, and they likewise freeze well for as long as a quarter of a year.

Nutrition:

Cal: 70

Carbs: 22g

Net Carbs: 2.5 g

Fiber: 4.5 g

Fat: 8 g

Protein: 8 g

Sugars: 3 g

Cauliflower Tortillas Bread

Preparation Time: 6 minutes

Cooking time: 21 min

Serving: 5

Ingredients:

- 3/4 huge head cauliflower (or two cups riced)
- 2 huge eggs (Vegans, sub flax eggs)
- 1/4 cup cleaved crisp cilantro
- 1/2 medium lime, squeezed and zested
- Salt and pepper, to taste

Directions:

1. Preheat the stove to 375 degrees F., and line a heating sheet with material paper.

2. Trim the cauliflower cut it into little, uniform pieces, and heartbeat in a nourishment processor in groups until you get a couscous-like consistency. The finely riced cauliflower should make around 2 cups pressed.

3. Place the cauliflower in a microwave-safe bowl and microwave for 2 minutes, at that point mix and microwave again for an additional 2 minutes. In the event that you don't utilize a microwave, a steamer works similarly also. Spot the cauliflower in a fine cheesecloth or thin dishtowel and crush out however much fluid as could be expected, being mindful so as

not to consume yourself. Dishwashing gloves are recommended as it is boiling.

4. In a medium bowl, whisk the eggs. Include cauliflower, cilantro, lime, salt, and pepper. Blend until all around consolidated. Utilize your hands to shape 6 little "tortillas" on the material paper.

5. Bake for 10 minutes, cautiously flip every tortilla and come back to the stove for an extra 5 to 7 minutes, or until totally set. Spot tortillas on a wire rack to cool marginally.

6. Heat a medium-sized skillet on medium. Spot a prepared tortilla in the container, pushing down somewhat, and dark-colored for 1 to 2 minutes on each side. Rehash with residual tortillas.

Nutrition:

Cal: 30

Carbs: 8g

Net Carbs: 2.5 g

Fiber: 7.5 g

Fat: 8 g

Protein: 10g

Herb Focaccia Bread

Preparation Time: 3.5 hours

Cooking time: 45 minutes

Servings: 8

Ingredients:

Dough:

- 1 cup water
- 2 tablespoons canola oil
- 1 teaspoon salt
- 1 teaspoon dried basil
- 3 cups bread flour
- 2 teaspoons bread machine yeast

Topping:

- 1 tablespoon canola oil
- ½ cup fresh basil
- 2 cloves garlic (to taste)
- 2 tablespoons grated parmesan cheese
- 1 pinch salt
- 1 tablespoon cornmeal (optional)

Directions:

1. Put all of the bread ingredients in your bread machine, in the order listed above starting with the water, and finishing with the yeast. Make a well in middle of the flour and place the yeast in the well. Make sure the well doesn't touch any liquid. Set the bread machine to the dough function.

2. Check on the dough after about 5 minutes and make sure that it's a soft ball. Add water 1 tablespoon at a time if it's too dry, and add flour 1 tablespoon at a time if it's too wet.

3. When dough is ready put it on a lightly floured hard surface. Cover the dough and let it rest for 10 minutes.

4. While the dough is resting, chop up the garlic and basil, grease a 13x9 inch pan and evenly distribute cornmeal on top of it.

5. Once the dough has rested, press it into the greased pan. Drizzle oil on the dough and evenly distribute the salt parmesan, garlic, and basil.

Nutrition:

Calories: 108

Carbs: 37.4 g

Fiber: 1.6 g
Fat: 7.3 g
Protein: 7.7 g.

Cranberry Bread

Preparation Time: 10 minutes

Cooking time: 15 minutes

Serving: 20

Ingredients:

- 2 cups almond flour
- ½ cup erythritol
- 1 ½ tsp. baking powder
- ½ tsp. baking soda
- 1 tsp. salt
- 4 tbsps. Coconut oil
- 1 tsp. nutmeg, ground
- 4 eggs
- ½ cup coconut milk
- 12 Oz cranberries

Directions:

1. Add wet ingredients to bread machine pan.
2. Add dry ingredients to bread machine pan.
3. Set bread machine to the gluten free setting.
4. When it is ready, remove the pan from the machine.
5. Let cool slightly before transferring to a cooling rack.
6. You can store your bread for up to 5 days.

Nutrition:

Calories: 127

Carbohydrates: 10g

Protein: 3g

Fat: 11g

Basil Cheese Bread

Preparation Time: 5 minutes

Cooking time: 15 minutes

Servings: 10

Ingredients

- Almond flour, two cups
- Warm water, one cup
- Salt, half a teaspoon
- Basil dried, one teaspoon
- Half cup of mozzarella shredded cheese
- Quarter tsp. Of active dry yeast
- 3 tsp. Of melted unsalted butter
- 1 tsp. Of stevia powder

Directions

1. In a mixing container, combine the almond flour, dried basil, salt, shredded mozzarella cheese, and stevia powder.
2. Get another container, where you will combine the warm water and the melted unsalted butter.
3. As per the instructions on the manual of your machine, pour the ingredients in the bread pan, taking care to follow how to mix in the yeast.
4. Place the bread pan in the machine, and select the sweet bread setting, together with the crust type, if

available, then press start once you have closed the lid of the device.

5. When the bread is ready, using oven mitts, remove the bread pan from the machine. Use a stainless spatula to extract the bread from the pan and turn the pan upside down on a metallic rack where the bread will cool off before slicing it.

Nutrition:

Calories: 124

Fat: 8g

Carb: 2g

Protein: 11g

Cheesy Garlic Bread

Preparation Time: 30 minutes

Cooking time: 20 minutes

Serves: 10

Ingredients:

- 3/4 cup mozzarella, shredded
- 1/2 cup almond flour
- 2 tbsp. cream cheese
- 1 tbsp. garlic, crushed
- 1 tbsp. parsley
- 1 tsp baking powder
- Salt, to taste
- 1 egg
- For the toppings:
- 2 tbsp. melted butter
- 1/2 tsp. parsley
- 1 tsp. garlic clove, minced

Directions:

1. Mix together your topping ingredients and set aside.
2. Pour the remaining wet ingredients into the bread machine pan.
3. Add the dry ingredients.
4. Set bread machine to the gluten free setting.

5. When the bread is done, remove bread machine pan from the bread machine.
6. Let cool slightly before transferring to a cooling rack.
7. Once on a cooling rack, drizzle with the topping mix.
8. You can store your bread for up to 7 days.

Nutrition:

Calories: 29

Carbohydrates: 1g

Protein: 2g

Fat: 2g

No Corn Cornbread

Preparation Time: 10 minutes

Cooking time: 20 minutes

Servings: 8

Ingredients:

- ½ cup almond flour
- ¼ cup coconut flour
- ¼ tsp. salt
- ¼ tsp. baking soda
- 3 eggs
- ¼ cup unsalted butter
- 2 Tbsp. low-carb sweetener
- ½ cup coconut milk

Directions:

1. Preheat the oven to 325F. Line a baking pan.
2. Combine dry ingredients in a bowl.
3. Put all the dry ingredients to the wet ones and blend well.
4. Dispense the batter into the baking pan and bake for 20 minutes.
5. Cool, slice, and serve.

Nutrition:

Calories: 65

Fat: 6g

Carb: 2g

Protein: 2g

CPSIA information can be obtained
at www.ICGtesting.com
Printed in the USA
LVHW020938260521
688445LV00005B/530